TO: _____

FROM: _____

PRESENT THIS COUPON TO REDEEM

One Full-Body Massage

VALID FOR ONE UNTIL FOREVER*

*TERMS AND CONDITIONS APPLY

PRESENT THIS COUPON TO REDEEM

One Naughty Session

VALID FOR ONE UNTIL FOREVER*

PRESENT THIS COUPON TO REDEEM

One Breakfast In Bed

VALID FOR ONE UNTIL FOREVER*

*TERMS AND CONDITIONS APPLY

Laugh At One Joke

VALID FOR ONE UNTIL FOREVER*

*TERMS AND CONDITIONS APPLY

PRESENT THIS COUPON TO REDEEM

One Compliment

VALID FOR ONE UNTIL FOREVER*

*TERMS AND CONDITIONS APPLY

One Special Activity Request

VALID FOR ONE UNTIL FOREVER*

*TERMS AND CONDITIONS APPLY

PRESENT THIS COUPON TO REDEEM

One Homemade Dinner

VALID FOR ONE UNTIL FOREVER*

*TERMS AND CONDITIONS APPLY

PRESENT THIS COUPON TO REDEEM

One Cuddle Session

VALID FOR ONE UNTIL FOREVER*

*TERMS AND CONDITIONS APPLY

PRESENT THIS COUPON TO REDEEM

One Public Show of Praise

VALID FOR ONE UNTIL FOREVER*

*TERMS AND CONDITIONS APPLY

PRESENT THIS COUPON TO REDEEM

One Night Out

VALID FOR ONE UNTIL FOREVER*

*TERMS AND CONDITIONS APPLY

PRESENT THIS COUPON TO REDEEM

One Session of Emotional Support

VALID FOR ONE UNTIL FOREVER*

*TERMS AND CONDITIONS APPLY

PRESENT THIS COUPON TO REDEEM

One Household Chore

VALID FOR ONE UNTIL FOREVER*

*TERMS AND CONDITIONS APPLY

PRESENT THIS COUPON TO REDEEM

One Love Note

VALID FOR ONE UNTIL FOREVER*

*TERMS AND CONDITIONS APPLY

PRESENT THIS COUPON TO REDEEM

One Naughty Request

VALID FOR ONE UNTIL FOREVER*

PRESENT THIS COUPON TO REDEEM

One Special Date Night

VALID FOR ONE UNTIL FOREVER*

PRESENT THIS COUPON TO REDEEM

One Netflix & Chill

VALID FOR ONE UNTIL FOREVER*

*TERMS AND CONDITIONS APPLY

PRESENT THIS COUPON TO REDEEM

One Costume Request

VALID FOR ONE UNTIL FOREVER*

*TERMS AND CONDITIONS APPLY

PRESENT THIS COUPON TO REDEEM

One Head Massage

VALID FOR ONE UNTIL FOREVER*

*TERMS AND CONDITIONS APPLY

PRESENT THIS COUPON TO REDEEM

One Spontaneous Sexy Time

VALID FOR ONE UNTIL FOREVER*

*TERMS AND CONDITIONS APPLY

PRESENT THIS COUPON TO REDEEM

One Gesture of Gratitude

VALID FOR ONE UNTIL FOREVER*

*TERMS AND CONDITIONS APPLY

PRESENT THIS COUPON TO REDEEM

One Listening Session

VALID FOR ONE UNTIL FOREVER*

*TERMS AND CONDITIONS APPLY

PRESENT THIS COUPON TO REDEEM

One Lunch Date

VALID FOR ONE UNTIL FOREVER*

*TERMS AND CONDITIONS APPLY

PRESENT THIS COUPON TO REDEEM

One Lovemaking Session

VALID FOR ONE UNTIL FOREVER*

*TERMS AND CONDITIONS APPLY

PRESENT THIS COUPON TO REDEEM

One Errand

VALID FOR ONE UNTIL FOREVER*

*TERMS AND CONDITIONS APPLY

PRESENT THIS COUPON TO REDEEM

Words of Encouragement

VALID FOR ONE UNTIL FOREVER*

*TERMS AND CONDITIONS APPLY

PRESENT THIS COUPON TO REDEEM

One Homemade Dessert

VALID FOR ONE UNTIL FOREVER*

*TERMS AND CONDITIONS APPLY

PRESENT THIS COUPON TO REDEEM

One Getaway Trip

VALID FOR ONE UNTIL FOREVER*

*TERMS AND CONDITIONS APPLY

PRESENT THIS COUPON TO REDEEM

One Special Bedroom Request

VALID FOR ONE UNTIL FOREVER*

PRESENT THIS COUPON TO REDEEM

Win One Argument

VALID FOR ONE UNTIL FOREVER*

*TERMS AND CONDITIONS APPLY

PRESENT THIS COUPON TO REDEEM

One Long Hug

VALID FOR ONE UNTIL FOREVER*

*TERMS AND CONDITIONS APPLY

Printed in Great Britain
by Amazon

33344951R00035